THE PSALMS

The Psalms

An Emerging Image of God

Thomas P. Rausch, SJ

Paulist Press
New York / Mahwah, NJ

Cover image by JS CHENYU ARTS / Shutterstock.com
Cover and book design by Lynn Else

Library of Congress Cataloging-in-Publication Data available upon request.

ISBN 978-0-8091-5767-9 (paperback)
ISBN 978-0-8091-8933-5 (ebook)

Published by Paulist Press
997 Macarthur Boulevard
Mahwah, NJ 07430
www.paulistpress.com

Printed and bound in the
United States of America

For all my Cistercian friends
at New Clairvaux,
with us and beyond,
in appreciation

Be still and know that I am God!

Psalm 46:11

CONTENTS

FOREWORD

As Fr. Thomas Rausch highlights in chapter 4 of this book, monastic women and men like me have prayed the psalms from the earliest years of Christianity. Prior to the liturgical renewal of Vatican II, the Abbey of Gethsemani in Kentucky had the tradition of chanting in choir on Good Friday the entire Psalter of 150 psalms without any break or intermission. This was seen as a special commemoration of the hours that Jesus spent, hanging on the cross, and lasted a good three and a half hours.

As a young monk at Gethsemani, I found this observance challenging. I was a scholastic at the time, a monk studying for the priesthood, and Fr. Thomas Merton was our director. I went to Merton to express how difficult I found this long chanting of 150 psalms. He listened, then responded simply how he found that chanting the psalms in this manner, as one integral unit, gave him a new insight into the mystery of Christ. I have always remembered his response and have striven to see the psalms and the way they speak of God—their image of God, as foundational to the mystery of Christ.

This book, *The Psalms*, is remarkable in that it leads into the mystery of God, a mystery that is at the heart of modern theology stemming from Vatican II. Theology is simply ways of speaking about the mystery of God. The way to speak about God is a current issue and the psalms are at the heart of this issue, for they present exceptional images of the mystery of God. Our personal dedication to praying the psalms in tandem with a radical inner openness makes it possible for us to pass through this way of speaking about the mystery of God, limited as it is by language, into a contemplative stance of awe in the presence of this unseen God—divinity, itself—working in our lives and in creation.

The truth that God wants us to know who and what God is we find referenced within the scriptures themselves. The basic revelation in the psalms is brought to fulfillment by Christ's own revelation. The twenty-fourth chapter of the Gospel according to Luke recounts the risen Christ as interpreting the scriptures, first to the two disciples on their way to Emmaus and then later that same day, the evening of his resurrection, to the twelve. The purpose being that they understand who and what he is, the God of the scriptures. These scriptures are the Old Testament and undoubtedly the psalms were included because they are essential to providing an image of God.

Furthermore, the twentieth chapter of the Gospel according to John provides nuance to an even earlier event of a similar nature on that same day of resurrection. Mary Magdalene announces to Peter and the other disciple that she had found the tomb of Jesus empty. These two disciples run to the tomb, and when the other disciple enters the tomb, he sees and believes. While the Gospel does not say what he believes, a safe conjecture would be that he recalls the words of Jesus that he would rise after three days. The Gospel continues on to reveal that these disciples do not yet understand the God of the scriptures. This Gospel passage can be interpreted as making a good distinction between belief and understanding as to who and what Jesus reveals himself to be, now glorified in his Paschal Mystery.

The risen Jesus giving his apostles insight into the scriptures is a first instance of comprehensive understanding the implications of the God of the Psalmist. This insight both brings to fulfillment the revelation of the God of the Psalmist, now in the context of the mystery of Christ, and inaugurates a change that will affect the disciples' lives in a most radical manner.

It might seem odd to some persons that the insights contained in the chapters of this book, titled "A Transcendent God," "Creator of Heaven and Earth," and "A God Who Saves his People," could be foundational to the mystery of Christ. Yet this is the very revelation that the risen Christ makes to his disciples on the day of resurrection and pours forth more dramatically on the day of Pentecost. These chapters incarnate, so to speak, the life of Jesus. The Prologue to the Gospel according to John captures this same marvelous mystery. It intimates that the image of God in the psalms, revealed as the Living Word of God, is also the Divine Logos of the New Testament in the person of Jesus Christ. It is a magnificent integration of the two scriptural Testaments for persons of Christian belief.

This book on the psalms offers a penetrating insight into *who* and *what* God is according to the psalms. Such a revelation presents for many persons the possibility of different ways to understand God, a new vision of divinity.

The chapters of this book elaborate the Hebrew concept of "Blessed be God," an important concept that calls our attention to God's revelation through God's direct involvement with and acting in creation and human life. This is the image of God found in the psalms. Today, this involvement and acting is referred to as "Divine Providence," the "Will of God," and other similar expressions. The psalms challenge persons praying them to embrace willingly this image and its vision of God and the consequence of this vision. They foster an intimate bonding with this God of the Psalmist who is present and acting in every aspect of creation and human life. This powerful belief brings forth the goodness present in human life while admitting the violence and anger in human hearts that the so-called imprecating psalms speak of and elaborate, invoking God's righteous judgment. If we view them as expressive of those passions, thoughts, and desires that constitute evil present in the depths of a human heart, as did many of the fathers of the Church, the imprecating psalms can unlock the way to authentic self-knowledge vital to conversion and bonding with the God of the psalms.

The last chapter of this book is dedicated to ways the psalms have been and are being used individually and communally. Persons living the Benedictine way of life are dedicated to the *Opus Dei*, the work of God. Benedict chose this term to describe the monastic responsibility of communally daily chanting the psalms that is essential for preparing for contemplation. This embracing the psalms and their content as the work of God is in the Hebraic tradition of acknowledging all creation and human activity to be expressive of God's revealing presence at work in human life and creation. Christian tradition accepts this approach with the belief that this Divine Presence is the Logos or Christ Incarnate, God with us. The psalms, pregnant with the Divine Presence, became the prayer of Christ, who is the image of the unseen God, the *who* and *what* of God's Work. Such is the core reason to pray the psalms: to experience God's self-revelation.

Fr. Rausch, a well-known theologian and author, has been joining us to chant the psalms on his yearly retreats here at the Abbey of New Clairvaux in Vina, California for about fifty years. As I read through his presentation of the psalms' profound understanding of God, I was amazed, appreciating his succinct, precise, insightful, and intelligent arrangement of the various academic studies that could be rather daunting for a person desiring to become acquainted with the psalms. By speaking and singing about their relationship with God, the psalms speak the very Living Word of God. Fr. Rausch clarifies their speaking of the Word of God and connects it with its profound consequences. This way, speaking the Living Word of God, invites us to participate in a relationship with God's image. Speaking from experience, this relationship, while prayerful, can be puzzling and challenging. But in accord with our participation, there will be awe-inspiring contemplative moments—rare, but they do happen—that carry us beyond a rational understanding into an intimate bonding with and knowing of the God of the Psalmist.

Thomas X. Davis, OCSO
Abbey of New Clairvaux

ACKNOWLEDGMENTS

The psalms are rich in human emotion. Full of praise before the beauty of God's creation, calling out to God in times of need, mourning a broken friendship or betrayal, or simply expressing a longing to experience God's presence, they invite us into prayer. "The LORD is my shepherd, I shall not want" (Ps 23:1); "Bless the LORD, O my soul, and all that is within me, bless his holy name" (Ps 103:1); "Your face, LORD, do I seek, do not hide your face from me" (Ps 27:8–9). Holding on to a verse or an image so often brings comfort and hope.

I am familiar with the psalms both from their place in our liturgy and from praying the Divine Office each day. But making retreats with the monks at the Abbey of New Clairvaux over the years and hearing their plaintive chants long before dawn or at the end of the day has implanted the poetry of the psalms deep within my imagination. Often a phrase or image from the office will stay with me, providing a focus for the day's prayer. I am especially grateful to Father Thomas Davis, who was the abbot at New Clairvaux for thirty-eight years, for welcoming me on my visits there and graciously contributing the foreword to this book. Under Fr. Thomas's leadership, the "sacred stones" from an eight-hundred-year-old Cistercian abbey in Spain, Santa Maria de Óvila, brought to the United States in 1931 by William Randolph Hearst and for some sixty years stored in Golden Gate Park, were trucked to Vina, California, in 1994 and restored in what is now the abbey's church.

I am also grateful to my long-time friend and colleague Michael Downey for his review of the manuscript and for his many helpful suggestions, and to Paul McMahon, my editor and now president and publisher at Paulist Press, who has long improved my works with his careful editing. Psalms cited directly are taken from the New American Bible Revised Edition.

INTRODUCTION

I have long cherished the psalms and the view of the divine they celebrate. That the Israelites could develop such a profound idea of God, so different from the gods of the culture out of which they came, is fascinating: It suggests the reality of revelation.

Revelation is subtle. It is not dictated by God, to be interpreted literally as Christian fundamentalists do, nor does the Word of God literally become text as in Islam. Revelation is God's free self-disclosure. It is recognizable in nature and given witness in scripture. Biblical revelation is "the Word of God in the words of men." God's Spirit works through the insights of prophetic figures, helping them to see more deeply, awakening their imaginations, finding ways to express the mystery of the divine in story, metaphor, and symbol.

Revelation is frequently expressed in poetry and a poet's sensibility helps one to grasp its meaning. Christians recognize God's revelation preeminently in the person of Jesus—in his sayings and parables and in the events of his life. But the Old and New Testaments, the sacred texts of the Hebrew Bible and the Gospels and epistles of the first Christians are also important sources.

To read the psalms is to see Israel at prayer. As Sigmund Mowinckel argued, the setting for most of the psalms was the official liturgy or cult of Israel.[1] They were sung during processions into the temple or in the services that followed, accompanied by various instruments (cf. Ps 150). Some included directions for liturgical leaders (cf. Ps 118:1–4), added later to the psalm heading. Individuals also prayed the psalms. Woven through them is an almost Franciscan appreciation of nature: the beauty of the sun, the moon, and the stars; the changing of seasons; the mountains and valleys with streams watering the fields, making them fertile, producing food for all earth's creatures (cf. Ps 104). The psalms help us understand the rich religious imagination of the Israelite community.

For their prayer, they gathered in the temple, a sacred place where YHWH dwelt among his people. Some references to it are indirect, substituting "the shelter of God's wings," "the face of God," or "God's holy mountain" for the temple itself. To enter the temple was to come into God's presence (*shekhinah*), a joyful moment reflected in the psalms that appeal not only to the head, but also to the heart. For example, we read, "How lovely your dwelling place, O LORD of hosts! My soul yearns and pines for the courts of the LORD. My heart and flesh cry out for the living God" (Ps 84:2–3), or "I rejoiced when they said to me, 'Let us go to the house of the LORD'" (Ps 122:1).

Psalm 68 is a mixed hymn with various themes, but in describing a procession into the Temple, it gives us an insight into the temple liturgy: "Your procession comes into view, O God, your procession into the holy place, my God and king. The singers go first, the harpists follow; in their midst girls sound the timbrels" (Ps 68:25–26). Or again, "Shout joyfully to the Lord, all you lands; serve the LORD with gladness; come before him with joyful song" (Ps 100:1–2). Yet in calling attention to those who absent themselves, who say there is no God (cf. Pss 10:4; 14:1) or claim that he does not see those who do evil (cf. Ps 94:3–7), the psalms sound very contemporary.

Christian monks and nuns have echoed the Israelites, calling out to God in the evening, in the morning, and at noon (cf. Ps 55:18), praying or chanting the psalms since the earliest days of the Church. Originally called the Divine Office, many lay Christians pray them today as the *Liturgy of the Hours*. St. Ambrose, who helped bring St. Augustine into the Church, celebrated the richness of the psalms: "In the Book of Psalms there is profit for all, with healing power for our salvation. There is instruction from history, teaching from the law, prediction from prophecy, chastisement from denunciation, persuasion from moral preaching. All who read it may find the cure for their own individual failings."[2]

Thus, the psalms fall into different categories. There are hymns of praise, thanksgiving psalms, or wisdom psalms. Royal psalms focus on the king. In some of these, the king is the speaker; others are royal thanksgiving psalms, attributed to David or the king. Some are historical psalms, celebrating YHWH's great works for his people, entering a covenant, leading them out of Egypt, giving them food in the desert and water to drink, guiding them to the land of promise, and overcoming their enemies. Enthronement psalms ritually celebrate YHWH's rule over all Israel, all the nations, and creation itself, with "king" being one of his titles (cf. Pss 96—99).

Other psalms are laments, both individual and communal. There are about forty individual laments, more than any other kind of psalm. They express a longing for God's saving presence. "I lie awake and moan, like a lone sparrow on the roof. All day long my enemies taunt me; in their rage, they make my name a curse" (Ps 102:8–9). Many psalms end with a confession that God will hear their prayers and come to the assistance of the petitioner. For example, both Mark and Matthew see Jesus crying out from the cross: "My God, my God, why have you abandoned me," the opening verse of Ps 22 that sounds like a cry of despair, but ends with a conviction that God will hear the Psalmist's cry, and he will again offer God praise.

Some psalms are torah psalms that are meant to instruct. Using metaphors, Psalm 1 introduces the Book of the Psalms, laying down two ways of living. The way of the just yields fruit in due season, while the wicked are blown away like chaff before the wind. The very long Psalm 119 celebrates the wisdom and joy the faithful find in doing God's will, revealed in the law. In some psalms, God is portrayed as speaking directly to the people (cf. Pss 46:11; 81:8–16). The Davidic psalms are recognized today as more than simply historical; they are representative. David becomes everyman, a universalizing of their meaning that speaks to the hearts of many.

Historical Context

Though dating the psalms is difficult, they seem to have originated between the tenth and fifth centuries BCE. Divided into five "books," they were traditionally attributed to David, but his authorship is doubted by most today. Citations of the psalms in the New Testament are generally from the Septuagint (85 percent), the Greek translation of the Hebrew scriptures dating from the middle of the third century down to the second. While there are some minor differences between the two texts, since the discovery of the Dead Sea Scrolls it has been possible to compare many of the psalms in the Septuagint with the original Hebrew texts in developing a critical edition.

It is helpful to appreciate the context out of which the psalms come. The Israelites lived among the Canaanites, a polytheistic people whose gods, fashioned out of precious metals or stone, were often bloodthirsty deities representing forces of nature. Though an accurate reconstruction of Canaanite religious practice is difficult, what we know is largely based on clay tablets from Ugarit, a Canaanite port city in northern Syria. El was the high god of the Canaanite pantheon. Baal (*ba'al,* meaning owner or lord in Hebrew) was originally associated with ancient Hadad, the storm and fertility god in ancient Mesopotamian and Canaanite religion. Thus, for the Canaanites, Baal was the god of rain and fertility, usually said to be the son of Dagan, though some Ugaritic texts identify him as a son of El. His consort was Ashtoreth or Astarte. There were multiple Baals, as each Canaanite city had its own.

In the Baal myths, Baal was the most powerful of the gods; in Canaan, he gradually replaced El, who remained more distant. Baal struggles against Mot, the god of death who swallows him and sends him to the underworld. Without Baal, a terrible drought ensues. It is only when Anat, the virgin goddess of war, defeats Mot and scatters his remains that Baal is released, and the rains come again to water the earth. Baal also engaged in combat with other symbolic adversaries: Yam, the Canaanite sea god, and Leviathan (Lotan), the mythical sea-serpent that personifies the primeval waters of chaos. Another version appears in the Babylonian creation epic, the *Enuma Elish*, with its story of Marduk's epic battle against Tiamat. These watery adversaries have left their mark on the Old Testament, where YHWH is the conqueror.

Scholars traditionally held that Baal was worshipped by a fertility cult involving promiscuous sexual relations between temple priests and priestesses, sometimes involving others who joined it, an obvious scandal to the Israelites. Today, some scholars argue that this reflects Israelite bias, the only evidence being two biblical texts (cf. Deut 23:18; Gen 38:21–22). The question remains contentious. Still, fertility played an important role in Canaanite religion, as their numerous fertility figurines suggest.

In early Israel, there seems also to have been a woman's cult of Asherah, considered the chief wife of YHWH until the reform of Josiah (621 BCE). As Israel's understanding of God developed, any sexual dimensions were eliminated, and YHWH became not just a local deity but one who, without consort, ruled over all the nations and creation itself, thus a universal God.

Canaanite religious practice consisted of memorials to honor the dead, cereal offerings, animal sacrifices or "whole burnt offerings," and, in some cases, human sacrifices. Many religious historians believe that Israelite religious ideas grew out of their Canaanite background, and the study of ancient Near Eastern literature has enhanced our understanding of the psalms. But certainly, Israel had its own sources in figures like Moses and other prophetic teachers who shaped their tradition.

Images of God

False images of God are not just an ancient problem. Ideas about the divine today are often varied and frequently confused. Few reduce God to graven images like Israel's neighbors, but many see God as an ever-vigilant disciplinarian, waiting for us to step out of line. That was certainly my idea as a child, at an earlier age in the Church. Deists believe in a divine lawgiver who establishes the universe and then lets it run according to its laws; while remaining at a distance; he doesn't intervene. Nor is their God personal.

Others allow for a distant God who created and ordered the world, wants people to be nice and fair to each other, be happy and feel good about themselves, but does not need to be particularly involved in their lives. Christian Smith and Melinda Lundquist Denton call this Moralistic Therapeutic Deism.[3] Living in God's grace does not seem to be a concern. Many young adults, when asked about their belief, refer to a vague "higher power," something like the

Force in the *Star Wars* series. But what they mean by this remains unclear.

What is suggested by these notions of the divine is far from the God of Christian revelation. The God who once centered our religious imaginations and played an important role in the development of Western culture seems to have faded from view. We live in what Charles Taylor has referred to as *a secular age*, stripped of its mystery and its hope.[4] Without a sense for the divine, religious demographics have changed significantly. Many Christians have joined the "nones," those who have left behind not only their churches, but also the faith itself. Social scientists are predicting that soon Christians will make up less than half of the U.S. population.

Thus, in this book, I explore the Psalmist's idea of God. The psalms are a particularly rich source. They proclaim a transcendent deity, a God who creates and sustains creation, who calls a people and enters a covenant relationship with them, rescuing them in times of trouble and guiding them with the help of prophetic figures. Two themes predominate; God is presented as both *creator* and *savior*. Other attributes of YHWH include his justice or righteous (*sedeq*) and mercy or loving kindness (*hesed*).

The psalms have much to teach us about the mystery of the divine. Jesus made frequent references to the psalms; the God he called *Abba* was the God of the Psalmist. Let's now explore the psalms more deeply.

1

A TRANSCENDENT GOD

The polytheistic religious culture of ancient Canaan was rich in gods, festivals, representative images, and fertility figures. Their holocausts, communion sacrifices, and cereal offerings influenced Israelite religious practice, while their mythological epics like Baal's victory over Yam and Mot, parallel to Marduk's victory over Tiamat, the monstrous sea-serpent who represented the primeval waters of chaos in the Babylonian creation epic, find frequent echoes in the Old Testament literature, including the psalms.

The idea of the divine that developed in Israel, however, was very different. The Israelite imagination was unlike the more abstract, philosophical mentality of the Greeks. The Psalmists used anthropomorphic and mythopoetic images to bring their idea of the divine to expression. Theirs was a God who creates the heavens and the earth and judges the earth from above. They confessed YHWH (Lord in English) as king, robed in majesty, with an everlasting throne. The clouds are God's chariot, and God travels on the wings of the wind and calls the stars by name. Looking down on the nations, judging with righteousness, God sharpens his sword and bends his bow to string it, preparing deadly shafts and making arrows blaze like thunderbolts.

Transcendence

YHWH's difference from the creatures of his world, his inability to be represented by idols of wood or stone, "graven images" according to the King James Bible (cf. Exod 20:4), or his transcendence in more philosophical language, is expressed by the word *holy*. The root for *holy*, the Hebrew root, *kdš*, has the basic meaning of separate, other, a quality unique to YHWH. It suggests difference, mystery, a moral and physical perfection. The Hebrew word for *holy*, *kadosh*, means separate, other, or sometimes consecrated. The psalms describe God as just and holy, and holy are his ways (cf. Pss 77:14; 99:9).

Thus, Israel's God was different from the gods of its neighbors. Like Moses before the burning bush, philosophers and theologians refer to the mysterious character of the divine, to the "wholly other" nature of God, as God's transcendence. While the biblical authors would probably not use such an abstract term to describe their God, they understood the mysterious nature of the divine.

Their God was unlike any creature. They praised God as high above all nations, with a glory above the heavens.

"Who," they asked, "is like the LORD our God, enthroned on high, looking down on heaven and earth?" (Ps 113:5–6). YHWH holds the nations to account: "[He] who judges the world with justice, who judges the peoples with fairness" (Ps 9:9). Different from created reality, God could be described and praised, but not materially represented. The Decalogue specifically forbids representational idols: "You shall not make for yourself an idol or a likeness of anything in the heavens above or on the earth below or in the waters beneath the earth" (Exod 20:4; cf. Deut 5:8).

The Psalmist mocks the gods of the Canaanites: "Their idols are silver and gold, the work of human hands. They have mouths but do not speak; eyes but do not see. They have ears, but do not hear; noses, but do not smell" (Ps 115:4–6; cf. 135:15–17). One hears the sarcasm in God's voice: "Were I hungry, I would not tell you, for mine is the world and all that fills it. Do I eat the flesh of bulls or drink the blood of he-goats?" (Ps 50:12–13). He rebukes them for exchanging the glory of God "for the image of a grass-eating bull" (Ps 106:20) and accuses them of sacrificing their sons and daughters to the idols of Canaan (cf. Ps 106:38).

Israel's God does not demand offerings of food and drink, nor does he desire sacrifices or burnt offerings, but ears that are open, symbolizing an obedient heart (cf. Ps 40:7). Most importantly, unlike the gods of the ancient world, the God of Israel demands ethical living. The Lord tests the righteous and hates the lover of violence; he will rain coals of fire and sulfur on the wicked (cf. Ps 11:5–6). To those who do evil, he says,

Why do you recite my commandments
  and profess my covenant with your mouth?
You hate discipline;
  you cast my words behind you!
If you see a thief, you run with him;
  with adulterers you throw in your lot.
    (Ps 50:16–18)

Psalm 119, the longest in the Psalter, is a celebration of "those whose way is blameless, who walk in the law of the LORD" (119:1). Thus, it is a psalm in praise of God's law, the *torah*—though, as Roland Murphy points out, *torah* here does not mean law in a narrow legal sense; "it is rather devotion to the divine will, the divine word, which for Israel was being continually actualized in its experience."[1] Repeatedly, it proclaims that to observe the law brings one joy and delight; it is better than riches (v. 14), better than thousands of gold and silver pieces (v. 72). "Your word is a lamp for my feet and a light for my path" (v. 105). Those who love the law have much peace (v. 165).

Immanent

But if the Psalmist's God is transcendent, beyond, God is also immanent: near or close. The psalms sing repeatedly of God's closeness to his people. YHWH is merciful and gracious, slow to anger, abounding in kindness. He rules over Judah, making the cities of Jacob rejoice. A stronghold for the oppressed, a rock of refuge in times of trouble, God hears the cry of the *anawim*: the poor or needy (cf. Pss 34:7; 69:34).

Most of the psalms proclaim God's unique relationship with Israel, but some of them are highly personal in their expression and suggest their use, not just liturgically but also in personal prayer. To become aware of God's love and nearness is to long for God's presence, to see his face. Psalm 42:1–2 expresses this desire of the heart:

> As the deer longs for streams of water,
> so my soul longs for you, O God.
> My soul thirsts for God, the living God.
> When can I enter and see the face of God?
> (42:1–2)

In this very personal hymn, the author remembers taking part in the temple worship and longs to do so again. This same theme continues into Psalm 43, often considered, with its predecessor, as constituting the second part of a single hymn. The author prays for God's light to lead him once more to the temple and its worship:

> That I may come to the altar of God,
> to God, my joy, my delight.
> Then I will praise you with the harp,
> O God, my God. (Ps 43:4)

Jerome's Vulgate translation of the psalm in the pre–Vatican II liturgy reads, "I will go unto the altar of God, unto God, who giveth joy to my youth;" a translation perhaps not precise, but beautiful nonetheless.

The language of Psalm 89 is also very personal. The psalm is a lament that reviews YHWH's covenant with

David, revealed in Nathan's oracle (cf. 2 Sam 7:12–16). The psalm begins, "I will sing of your mercy forever, LORD proclaim your faithfulness through all ages" (Ps 89:2). After praising God for his work in creation and reminding God of his promises to David and his descendants, the Psalmist complains that God seems to have forgotten his promises, suggesting an intimate relation with the divine. And it ends with the plea:

> Remember, Lord, the insults to your servants,
> how I have borne in my bosom the slander
> of the nations.
> Your enemies, Lord, insult;
> they insult each step of your anointed.
> (Ps 89:51–52)

The psalm refers frequently to God's steadfast love.

Psalm 103 is another beautiful hymn displaying this same personal and communal character. It begins personally, "Bless the LORD, my soul, all my being, bless his holy name!" (Ps 108:1) then takes on a communal voice to thank the Lord for all the blessings received. It praises God for his steadfast love and mercy, his compassion, forgiveness of transgressions and renewal of youth, promising an everlasting love for those who keep his covenant down the generations. Roland Murphy observes, "Although the perspective is Israelite, the reasons are pertinent to all humanity, which is made from dust, like grass (Pss 37:2; 90:5; Isa 40:7)."[2] No wonder so many have found the psalms leading so easily to prayer.

A Contemporary Reflection

The Psalmist has a sense for the mystery of the divine. But how to describe God's otherness. Our language tends to break down. In Psalm 46, praising God for his saving presence through natural and military crises, the Psalmist interrupts himself to say in God's name, "Be still and know that I am God!" (Ps 46:11). Other biblical writers use the metaphors of light and darkness to try to express the luminosity and hiddenness of the holy. The Old Testament describes God as hidden in a "dark cloud" (Exod 20:21) or concealed by a cloud (cf. Exod 24:15–18).

Christian authors used similar language. The author of 1 Timothy says that God dwells in "unapproachable light" (1 Tim 6:16). Gregory of Nyssa (335–395) speaks of God hidden in a "luminous darkness." Anselm of Canterbury (1033–1109) returns to 1 Timothy's language and develops it: "Surely, Lord, inaccessible light is your dwelling place, for no one apart from yourself can enter it and fully comprehend you. If I fail to see this light, it is simply because it is too bright for me. Still, it is by this light that I do see all that I can, even as weak eyes, unable to look straight at the sun, see all that can be seen by the sun's light."[3] A fourteenth-century English text on contemplative prayer, acknowledging the divine transcendence, was entitled *The Cloud of Unknowing*.

Rudolph Otto identified the holy with the numinous, the "wholly other" as a quality of the divine, describing it as the *mysterium tremendum et fascinans*, a mysterious presence that both fascinates and frightens.[4] Karl Rahner referred to God's transcendence, so far beyond our ability to comprehend or imagine, as God's incomprehensibility.[5] But his understanding here involves far more than a sense for the divine mystery.

In speaking of God's incomprehensibility, Rahner refers to the great thirteenth-century Dominican theologian, Thomas Aquinas. According to Aquinas, God remains incomprehensible to finite intellects: our own and, for him, those of the angels, even in the immediacy of the "beatific" vision. He attributes this to the disproportion that continues to exist even in the beatific vision between the infinite self-communication of God and the finite intellect, even though illuminated by grace. For Aquinas, this does not stem from our distance from God, nor from a supposed negative quality of the divine, nor from some ignorance remaining even in the beatific vision, but is an aspect of the very nature of God. In the immediacy of the beatific vision, what is encountered is not a part of God, but the totality of God in his utter simplicity. This is not an opinion for Aquinas, but a doctrine of the faith. He points to several scriptural texts, especially to a verse in Romans, as the locus classicus where Paul writes: "Oh, the depth of the riches and wisdom and knowledge of God! How inscrutable are his judgments and how unsearchable his ways!" (Rom 11:33).

Rahner then turns paradoxically to the anthropological to argue that if God is transcendent, so also is man a question for which there is no answer, for each person as human subject has an unlimited transcendentality. As "spirit in the world," the human subject in knowing reaches beyond every object known, never reaching a complete fulfillment as we experience the infinite horizon that our questioning uncovers. He speaks of it as a transcendence into apparent emptiness, a transcendentality tending toward the incomprehensible that it wants to reach. Of course, one can close oneself to this unfulfilled desire. But if there is any answer to the question of who or what the human person is, it must be for Rahner "the worshipful love of God"[6] that alone is its fulfillment, to which it must surrender in love as Jesus did. If God is transcendent and incomprehensible, so is the human person with his or her unfulfilled transcendentality.

From this sense of the divine mystery—so close and yet so far—was to develop the rich contemplative tradition in the life of the Church. Augustine of Hippo sensed this mystery disclosed in the restlessness of our hearts; he finds traces of the mystery in our memories that lead us to search for the divine. In his *Confessions*, he describes this intimate presence of God, who is more present to us than we are to ourselves (cf. III,6,11). It is this intimacy that plants deep within us a desire for God; he writes that "our hearts are made for you O Lord, and they will not rest until they rest in you" (1,1).

Yet we can too easily distract ourselves and dull that longing with the pursuit of other creatures, as Augustine says in what is perhaps the most famous passage in the story of his conversion: "Late have I loved you, O Beauty ever ancient, ever new, late have I loved you! You were within me, but I was outside, and it was there that I searched for you. In my unloveliness I plunged into the lovely things which you created. You were with me, but I was not with you. The lovely things kept me far from you, though if they did not have their existence in you, they had no existence at all" (*Confessions*, X,27).

Apophatic and Cataphatic Mysticism

So how do we approach the God of steadfast love and compassion so beautifully described in the psalms? Those who write on Christian spirituality usually tend to one of two theological approaches to the divine mystery. One is apophatic theology; the other is cataphatic (or kataphatic) theology. Apophatic theology, also called negative theology, is rooted in the *mystical theology* of the late fifth- or early sixth-century theologian and philosopher known as Pseudo-Dionysius the Areopagite. Dionysius acknowledged that God can be described analogously with certain perfections of the natural order, thus as all-powerful, loving, good, and so on. At the same time, recognizing the transcendent nature of the divine, Dionysius argues that God is more appropriately approached by the *via negativa*, denying those predicates because the divine transcendence places God beyond any kind of being.

What emerges from his thought is the necessity of both approaches: one of affirmation; the other of negation. For while we affirm certain perfections of the divine, as indeed we find in the psalms, God remains mystery, ultimately unknowable. Thomas Aquinas, the Angelic Doctor, made this explicit. He taught that, although we cannot know God adequately, we can know something about God with the help of analogies drawn from the perfections of created reality.

Contemplation from the perspective of the apophatic tradition stresses an emptying of the minds of ideas and images and an attentive waiting or loving attentiveness to the God grasped in faith, but not sensed or experienced directly. It calls for a resting of the intellect and quieting of the senses, to enter the darkness that hides God's presence. Spiritual writers in the Eastern tradition stressing the importance of the *via negativa* include Gregory of Nyssa, John Chrysostom, and Basil the Great; contemporary examples would be John Meyendorff and Georges Florovsky. Western examples would include John Scotus Erigena, Meister Eckhart, and John of the Cross. Eckhart, the fourteenth-century Dominican, once said that "nothing in creation resembles God more than silence." John of the Cross, rejecting all visual and auditory experiences, described contemplation as an entering with a loving attentiveness into the dark night, or really, two dark nights. The first is the dark night of the senses, as there is no object for our senses to grasp. The dark night of the spirit refers to the divine transcendence that frustrates our intelligence, as it is so far beyond our ability to understand.

Two contemporary Trappists, Thomas Merton and Thomas Keating, have encouraged a contemplation that moves beyond images and rational meditation. In his beautiful *Seeds of Contemplation*, Merton wrote: "As soon as there is any reasonable indication that God is drawing the spirit into this way of contemplation, we ought to remain at peace in a prayer that is utterly simplified, stripped of acts and reflections and clean of images, waiting in emptiness and vigilant expectancy for the will of God to be done in us."[7] The title of the book echoes the "seeds of contemplation" that he describes so lyrically throughout the book: experiences of nature or of God's word, an unfamiliar truth that frees us from desires that holds us captive, or even the clamor of the city that awakens us to God's mysterious presence, like the poetry and metaphors we find so often in the psalms.

Keating has done much to popularize "centering prayer," a first step to contemplation. It involves sitting in silence for twenty or thirty minutes, not changing positions, resting quietly, disregarding any thoughts, feelings, or exercises of the imagination in the darkness that cloaks the Creator and Lord, the indwelling God present below the river of our consciousness. To stay focused, he suggests choosing a sacred word, a symbol of God's presence, something brief such as God, Abba, or Jesus. When one's usual flow of thoughts surfaces, one simply returns to the word. At the end of the period, one takes a minute or two to return to one's ordinary conscious awareness, perhaps finishing with some vocal prayer.[8] To disregard our thoughts and the images that fill our imaginations or to leave behind the false self of our often-conflicted feelings is to open ourselves to God's presence within.

Cataphatic prayer is more active; it makes use of images, symbols, feelings, and imagination to raise one's thoughts and affections to God. A sense for nature, its beauty, abundance, and vitality can bring many to an awareness of God. Saint Francis of Assisi, with his love for all God's creatures, including the poor, is an example of this kind of prayer.

Francis easily found God's presence in nature. He numbered all the animals among his brothers and sisters, preaching to the birds and, in a famous story, taming with his gentle approach a ravenous wolf who was terrorizing the Umbrian city of Gubbio. His beautiful *Canticle of the Sun* praises God for all his creatures, addressing them as Brother Sun, Sister Moon, Brother Wind, Sister Water, Brother Fire, and Mother Earth who sustains us, producing fruits, flowers, and herbs, even our Sister Bodily Death, from whom none can escape. Saint Francis is the patron saint of animals, birds, and the environment. The late Pope Francis, who chose his name to remind him of the poor, cites Francis at the beginning of his encyclical *Laudato Si'*, pleading for all to hear both the cry of the earth and the cry of the poor (no. 49).

In his *Spiritual Exercises*, St. Ignatius of Loyola encouraged the retreatants to pray with their imaginations, but he was not the first do so. St. Bonaventure encouraged others, including his Franciscan brothers, to pray over the life of Christ imaginatively. So did the Carthusian Ludolf of Saxony in a work that Inĩgo (Ignatius's given name) may have read during his recovery from his wounded leg in the Castle Loyola. Ignatius counseled his retreatants to imagine the different scenes in the life of Christ, even placing themselves within them.

Thus, he suggests that the retreatant begin a contemplation with a prelude, setting the scene. For example, in his contemplation on the Nativity, he asks the retreatant "to form a mental image of the scene and to see in my imagination the road from Nazareth to Bethlehem. I will consider its length and breadth, and whether it is level or winding through valleys and over hills. I will also behold the place of the cave of the Nativity, whether it is large or small, whether high or low, and what it contains."[9]

These exercises are more than simply a way of preparing for prayer. To imagine the gospel scenes in their concreteness and drama, to encounter the persons and even interact with them, is to be moved by the humanity of the persons in these gospel stories in a way that resonates with our own. Contemplating Jesus choosing his disciples, caring for others, or in his suffering touches not only our intellect but our feelings, embedding the scene in our affective memory.

While we may be drawn to focus more on one than another of these approaches to prayer, we can use whichever is most helpful to enter prayer. Mother Teresa of Calcutta certainly was familiar with both. In her early days as a Sister of Loreto, she speaks of the joy she felt in serving the poorest of the poor. She was happy in her religious vocation and had an active, affective spiritual life. But that was to change. In 1946, after a mystical encounter with Christ on a train to Darjeeling for her annual retreat, she heard him calling her to leave all behind and to give herself entirely to ministry in the slums. Her work prospered, as other women joined her in what would become the congregation of the Missionaries of Charity.

But before long, she began to experience long years of darkness and pain, longing for God who seemed to be absent. She wrote to one of her spiritual directors, "Since 49 or 50 this terrible sense of loss—this untold darkness—this loneliness—this continual longing for God—which give me that pain deep down in my heart.—Darkness is such that I really do not see—neither with my mind nor with my reason—the place of God in my soul is blank.—There is no God in me—when the pain of longing is so great."[10] Her spiritual directors helped her to understand that her suffering was a share in the Passion of Christ, and she remained convinced of her union with God. But the experience was one of darkness. She lived in the dark night.

Conclusion

The God of Israel was far from being the stern judge so prevalent in popular Christianity. But the Israelites' God was also different from the violent gods of their Mesopotamian and Canaanite neighbors, mocked by the Psalmist as gods made by human hands.

Originally, the Israelites shared their polytheism. It took time for their monotheistic understanding of God to develop. YHWH was surrounded by a heavenly court (cf. Ps 29:1). Still, their God reigned alone, above the other gods (cf. Ps 82:1). These gods did not compare with Israel's God (cf. Ps 77:14). "Truly, who is God except the LORD? Who but our God is the rock?" (Ps 18:32; cf. Exod 15:11). Only the fool says there is no God (cf. Pss 15:1; 53:2).

The God the Israelites invoked in their worship and praised in their songs was an all-powerful deity, a holy God, beyond representation in handcrafted images. If they were moving beyond a God invoked with the blood of sacrificial animals, their God demanded righteousness of his people. In more contemporary terms, Israel's God was transcendent.

Israel's sense for the otherness or transcendence of God is reflected also in the Christian tradition that understands God as unknowable mystery, described with metaphors of darkness and light. Karl Rahner uses the language of incomprehensibility. Saint Augustine wrote that God leaves traces of his presence in our memories and in the restlessness of our hearts. Rahner describes the transcendental range of our intelligence that always reaches beyond the object known to sense the absolute, though in an unthematic way.

In approaching the divine mystery, Christian spirituality has used both approaches—the apophatic, the *via negativa* or way of negation, and the cataphatic, the *via positiva* or way of affirmation. The cataphatic tradition uses images, symbols, and the imagination to raise the heart and the mind to God, while the apophatic stresses emptying the senses and quieting the mind before the transcendent mystery of the divine. Both have eloquent advocates in the contemplative tradition.

2

CREATOR OF HEAVEN AND EARTH

The ancient Near East was not lacking in creation myths. Most of those describing human origins are based on a cosmogony; an epic battle of the gods. The *Atrahasis Epic*, named for its central character, dates from the eighteenth century BCE. It was discovered on several Akkadian cuneiform tablets. Tablet I begins with the story of a rebellion of the lesser gods who refuse their task of caring for their farms, canals, and rivers. In response, the greater gods, led by Anu, Enlil, and Enki, the gods of earth, wind, and water, decide to create humans to take their place. They fashion clay figurines, mixing them with the flesh and blood of a slain god. After gestating for ten months in a specially fashioned womb, human beings emerge. But they soon offend the gods by their noise and rapid spread.

In Tablet II, Enlil decides to send a great flood to destroy the troublesome humans. Tablet III tells the tale of how the hero, Atrahasis, escapes the deluge that follows, warned by Enki to tear down his house and build a boat. After he loads on it his family and animals, the rains begin. When they cease after seven days, Atrahasis disembarks and offers a sacrifice to the gods.

A later version of the story, the more familiar *Epic of Gilgamesh*, also tells the story of the great flood. Discovered in the Library of Ashurbanipal in ancient Nineveh, capital of Assyria (modern Mosul in Iraq) in the early 1850s, it begins with the story of Gilgamesh, who sets off on a journey to discover the secret of eternal life. On the way, he meets Utnapishtim, who with his wife are among the few survivors of the great flood. A later tablet recounts that story. Utnapishtim is ordered by Enki to build a great boat, seal it with pitch and bitumen, and go aboard with his family and "all the animals of the field." The storm lasts for six days, turning all the earth to clay and terrifying even the gods. When it ceases, the boat or ark comes to rest on a mountain and Utnapishtim sets free a dove, a swallow, and a raven. When the raven fails to return, he opens the ark and offers a sacrifice, receiving the gift of eternal life. The story is the basis for the Genesis account of the great flood or deluge. And other versions of the epic, with different heroes, are extent.

More familiar is the Babylonian *Enuma Elish* epic, discovered in 1849 on seven clay tablets and now also in the Library of Ashurbanipal. It tells the story of the creation of the gods, the visible world, and human beings. At its center is the great battle between Marduk, Babylon's god and patron of the city, and Tiamat, a dragon or serpent representing the formless but hostile primeval waters. Using the four winds and trapping Tiamat with a net when she attempts to swallow him, Marduk fills her with an evil wind, then shoots an arrow that pierces her heart. He splits her in two, using one half of her body to form the firmament or sky and the other the earth. He then makes the sun and the moon as stations for the gods, and makes the clouds and the rain, whose waters form the Tigris and Euphrates rivers. Finally, he makes human beings to serve the gods, fashioning them from the blood of one of the gods. As state and religion were closely linked, their service was necessary for the state's well-being.

Living in contact with the ancient cultures of Mesopotamia and Canaan, it should not be surprising that the Israelite religious literature would reflect that of their neighbors. The ancient battle between the ruling god and the watery chaos, symbolized by Marduk slaying Tiamat in the *Enuma Elish* epic or Baal overcoming Levithan, also appearing as Lotan or sometimes as Rahab or the Ugaritic god of the sea, Yam, in the ancient Baal cycle. This epic mythical battle with the forces of chaos has left frequent echoes in the biblical tradition. For example, the first Genesis creation story is not a creation from nothing (*creatio ex nihilo*), but imagines the earth as a "without form or shape (*tohu wa-vohu*)...and a mighty wind sweeping over the waters" (Gen 1:2); when God begins his creative work.

Other examples include Isaiah 27:1: "On that day, The LORD will punish with his sword that is cruel, great, and strong, Leviathan the fleeing serpent, Leviathan the coiled serpent; he will slay the dragon in the sea." Or Isaiah 51:9: "Was it not you who crushed Rahab, you who pierced the dragon?" (cf. Ps 89:10; Job 26:12). Also, Job 3:8: "Let them curse it who curse the Sea, those skilled at disturbing Leviathan!" Or Job 40:25 in the Hebrew text where the dragon is a crocodile: "Can you lead Leviathan about with a hook, or tie down his tongue with a rope?" Psalm 74:13–14 says, "You stirred up the sea by your might; you smashed the heads of the dragons on the waters. You crushed the heads of Leviathan, gave him as food to the sharks." In Psalm 104:26, the fearsome Leviathan has been defanged, reduced to a large fish that plays in YHWH's sea: "There ships ply their course and Leviathan, whom you formed to play with."

The most obvious similarities are to be found between the *Enuma Elish* epic and the first Genesis creation story, with numerous contacts if not a literary dependence. Both stories see a watery chaos present at the beginning, symbolized in the Babylonian version by Tiamat. Both envision the creation of the earth by a division of the primeval waters of chaos, Marduk splitting the body of Tiamat in the Babylonian account, Yahweh dividing the waters in Genesis. Some scholars contend that the word *deep* (*tehom* in Hebrew) is cognate with Tiamat, the primordial dragon in the Babylonian account. Both stories follow the same order of creation, and both refer to the day and night before the creation of the sun and the moon.

But how different are the two accounts of creation in Genesis, where God creates not by overcoming mythical creatures but by the sovereign power of the divine word (cf. Pss 33:6–9; 148:5). In the first Genesis creation account, God separates the waters to bring forth the earth simply by speaking: "Then God said: Let there be a dome in the middle of the waters, to separate one body of water from the other" (Gen 1:6).

Creator of Heaven and Earth

If the psalms echo the ancient conflict between Leviathan, symbolizing the watery chaos, they also offer a rich creation theology. Before the mountains were brought forth, YHWH formed the earth (cf. Ps 90), establishing it never to be moved (cf. Ps 93). He made the heavens (cf. Pss 33:6–9; 96; 102:25–27), the sun, the moon, and all the stars, all created at his command (cf. Pss 136; 148); he determined the number of the stars and calls each one by name (cf. Ps 147).

Psalm 148 is a hymn calling on all God's creatures to praise their Creator, the God who made the heavens above and the earth below, the sun, the moon, and the shining stars, fixing their boundaries. He made the seas and their creatures, the mountains and trees, wild animals, cattle, and birds, and all the people, the LORD whose name alone is exalted, whose glory is above both earth and heaven. Roland Murphy sees this psalm as standing behind Francis of Assisi's famous *Canticle of the Sun*.[1] This is YHWH, a personal God who made the earth and a people to be his own (cf. Ps 95), the one who formed the eye and the ear (cf. Ps 94).

Psalm 139 is a complex but very personal meditation or prayer:

> LORD, you have probed me, you know me:
> you know when I sit and stand;
> you understand my thoughts from afar.
> (Ps 139:1)

The Psalmist praises God for his constant and inescapable presence, his guiding hand, his intimate knowledge of the Psalmist and all he does, of what he will say long before he says it. He praises the God who formed his inward parts, who "knit me in my mother's womb" (v. 13), confessing that he is fearfully, wonderfully made as are all God's works. He knows that the days of his life are still hidden in God's book, ending with a prayer that God search him to see if there is any wickedness in his heart, asking that God lead him in the ways of his faithful ancestors.

God at Work in Creation

The God who created the heavens and the earth is not finished. Without using the more abstract language of immanence, the Psalmist sees God as active in history and in creation; intimately involved and sustaining it. God who silenced the roaring of the seas now waters the earth and makes it fruitful, covering the meadows with flocks and the valleys with grain (cf. Ps 65). Psalm 74 praises God for creating the sun and the luminaries, fixing the bounds of the earth and the seasons, imploring him to remember the lives of the poor. YHWH makes clouds to cover the earth, brings the winds out of his storehouses and lightning for the rain, making grass grow on the hills to provide food for the animals (cf. Pss 135; 147).

Psalm 104 is one of the most beautiful in the Psalter. Using poetic images, it opens with a description of God's ongoing work in creation, spreading the heavens out like a tent, riding on the clouds and the wind; YHWH sets the earth on its foundations and rebukes the waters of chaos with his thunder, lest they again cover the earth. The psalm then turns to YHWH's active care for the work of his hands. He waters the earth, giving his creatures streams of water to drink, causing grass to grow for the cattle, plants for people to use, oil to make their faces shine, bread for them to eat, and wine to warm their hearts.

God provides for each of the animals: cedar and fir trees for the birds to build their nests; high mountains for the wild goats; the moon to mark the seasons; darkness when the animals creep from the forests and the young lions roar for their prey, seeking their food from God. When the sun rises, they withdraw, and people go out to their work, to labor till evening falls. The Psalmist senses God's sustaining presence. He gives food to all his creatures, opening his hand to fill them with good things; when he sends forth his spirit they are created, and he renews the face of the earth. But when he hides his face, they die and return to dust. The psalm is a lovely hymn to creation and God's active presence within it.

In his "Contemplation to Attain Divine Love" at the end of his *Spiritual Exercises*, Saint Ignatius of Loyola presents a similar view of God enabling creation. He invites the retreatant to consider how God dwells in creatures, giving the elements being, the plants life, the animals sensation, and human beings understanding. Then he asks the retreatant "to consider how God works and labors for me in all created things on the face of the earth, that is, He conducts Himself as one who labors; in the heavens, the elements, plants fruits, flocks, etc. He gives them being, preserves them, grants them growth, sensation, etc."[2]

The Cosmic Christ

Too often, the popular view of creation is of something in the past, the work of a Deist God who fashions a world and then withdraws to let it run according to its laws, without further involvement on the part of the Creator. This is far from the biblical view. St. Paul's vision of God's salvation is not just anthropological, but cosmic. As early as 1 Corinthians, he writes,

> There is
> one God, the Father,
> from whom all things are and for whom we exist,
> and one Lord, Jesus Christ,
> through whom all things are and
> through whom we exist. (1 Cor 8:6)

Or in Colossians,

> He is the image of the invisible God,
> the firstborn of all creation.
> For in him were created all things in heaven and on earth,
> the visible and the invisible,
> whether thrones or dominions or
> principalities or powers;
> all things were created through
> him and for him. (Col 1:15–17)

In Romans, Paul sees not just humankind but even creation waiting for the fulness of salvation, waiting to be set free from its bondage to decay, hoping to obtain the glorious freedom of the children of God. "We know that all creation is groaning in labor pains even until now; and not only that, but we ourselves, who have the firstfruits of the Spirit, we also groan within ourselves as we wait for adoption, the redemption of our bodies" (Rom 8:22–23).

Like Paul, other New Testament authors see a fulfillment of humanity and creation itself in union with the risen Christ. John's Prologue speaks of the Word through whom all things came into being (cf. John 1:3) and at his final meal with his disciples, Jesus promises to gather his disciples again, after his death, in his Father's house (cf. John 14:2–5; Mark 14:25). The author of Revelation envisions a new heaven and a new earth, where God will make his home among us, wiping away every tear from our eyes and death will be no more (cf. Rev 21:1–4). In Jesus's name, he writes, "I am the Alpha and the Omega, the first and the last, the beginning and the end" (Rev 22:13).

Until that day, Christ must reign, "until he has put all his enemies under his feet," and "the last enemy to be destroyed is death....When everything is subjected to him, then the Son himself will [also] be subjected to the one who subjected everything to him, so that God may be all in all" (1 Cor 15:25–28).

A Contemporary Reflection

Some contemporary Christologies have moved in a different direction. Pluralist Christologies see Jesus not so much as the cause of salvation, but rather as its revealer or model. They are less likely to acknowledge the Word's role in creation. Praxis Christologies, emphasizing the social teaching of the historical Jesus, argue that one comes to know Christ only by imitating him. But some scholars, acknowledging a debt to the French Jesuit paleontologist and visionary, Teilhard de Chardin, and incorporating insights from their study of Charles Darwin and evolutionary science, have reclaimed the cosmic Christ of scripture. In a sense, they have recentered the work of Jesus as the creative Word of God within the Trinitarian mystery.

Teilhard envisioned a converging universe moving toward personalization and communion with Christ Omega, powered by the unitive power of love. While his vision may have been more mystical than strictly scientific, it is faithful to scripture. God's creative work takes place through the Word and in the Spirit. Creation begins and reaches its fulfillment in Christ. So, we could say that Incarnation and eschatology are correlative terms.

Other theologians have moved in similar directions. In his *Foundations of Christian Faith*, Karl Rahner sees a fundamental unity of spirit and matter. Though his approach differs from that of Teilhard, he argues that, since human beings as "spirit in the world" are oriented toward the absolute, an evolutionary perspective sees its ultimate fulfillment in the divinization of creation itself.[3] In his poetic ways, Pope Francis says something similar in his encyclical *Laudato Si'*, when he speaks of the Eucharist as cosmic:

> "Yes, cosmic! Because even when it is celebrated on the humble altar of a country church, the Eucharist is always in some way celebrated on the altar of the world." The Eucharist joins heaven and earth; it embraces and penetrates all creation. The world which came forth from God's hands returns to him in blessed and undivided adoration: in the bread of the Eucharist, "creation is projected towards divinization, towards the holy wedding feast, towards unification with the Creator himself." (*LS* 236)

John Haught sees evolution as a cosmic drama, sometimes tragic, with successes and failures as life in all its rich diversity struggles to be and to flourish. But in his *Making Sense of Evolution*, he recognizes a deeper coherence that Darwin fails to see. Like Teilhard de Chardin, who stresses a universe still unfinished, for Haught the universe is a work in progress. Creation is drawn forward by a God who, in becoming incarnate in Christ, animates creation through his Spirit toward a future he describes as the dwelling place of God. This is Haught's Trinitarian vision, a drama at the heart of the cosmic evolutionary process. Creation is moving toward its fulfillment in Christ so that, as Paul once said, God may be "all in all."[4]

In her book *Ask the Beasts*, Elizabeth Johnson argues that suffering and death is always part of the evolutionary process in all its abundance, and yet, in the vast epochs of time, God's creative Spirit is at work to accomplish God's purpose. It is into this world of cosmic development and common ancestry that the Word of God enters. She writes that it is in this "deep incarnation" that "the flesh assumed in Jesus Christ connects with all humanity, all biological life, all soil, the whole matrix of the material universe down to its very roots."[5] Rediscovering the cosmic Christ has revitalized Christology, frequently deconstructed by some liberal theologies.[6]

Conclusion

The psalms frequently draw on pagan sources, but in a way that transforms them. Not mythical gods in cosmic battles, but YHWH, the God of Israel, who creates by his sovereign power and watches benevolently over creation. In his goodness, God has brought order and beauty into the cosmos, taming the waters of chaos, creating a place for all his creatures, turning the fearsome Leviathan into a harmless fish. The Psalmist promises to sing to the LORD as long as he lives, ending with "Bless the LORD, my soul! Hallelujah!" (Ps 104:35).

God's creative work is ongoing, a *creatio continua.* The imagery is frequently poetic; the picture of God's world that emerges is lavish and beautiful. The Psalmist praises God's abundance in creation, his care for the earth: softening it with showers, watering it, blessing its growth, covering the hills with flocks and the valleys with grain so that the very meadows and pastures shout with joy (cf. Ps 65). Even the persistence of evil will not frustrate God's care.

The New Testament writers build on this imagery, seeing creation from a Trinitarian perspective. Creation is God's work through the continuing presence of the incarnate Word, the mediating agent of God's creativity and purpose, and in his animating, life-giving Spirit. Paul's Christology is both soteriological and cosmic; he sees humanity and creation itself finding its ultimate fulfillment in communion with the Trinitarian mystery when God will be all in all.

In the fourth Gospel, creation is in and through the Word that became flesh in Jesus of Nazareth who dwells in us with the Father and the Son. The visionary writer of Revelation sees a new heaven and a new earth, the work of Christ who is the Alpha and the Omega, the first and the last, the beginning and the end, a vision echoed in 2 Peter 3:13. So creation is not static; unfinished, it is moving forward animated by God's Spirit, drawn by the God of love whose love can move our hearts and bring us into communion with God and with each other.

In reflecting on the mystery of creation it is important to avoid two extremes: the *literalism* of the fundamentalist, and the *bleak world* of the scientific materialist. The fundamentalist, attempting to protect the biblical tradition from what is feared as the "slippery slope" of liberal theology, has difficulty recognizing how God's Spirit works through the imagination and personal experience of the biblical writers. The drama of human life too often escapes them. God appears as an all-powerful monarch, controlling a universe lacking genuine agency.

In some ways, the cosmos of materialists is similar. Their perspective is entirely material; human intelligence is not embodied spirit, but simply the product of physical processes in the brain, rooted in neurochemistry and the nervous system—neurological algorithms. The cosmos for the materialist is nothing more than the product of random molecular changes and chemical combinations. It has no future or destiny other than an irreversible decline into a state of inert uniformity, the grim view of the second law of thermodynamics or entropy. Materialists empty our vast and mysterious cosmos of spirit, design, and agency, reducing it to a Laplacian mechanism, a vast machine governed by mechanical principles, such that if the mass and motion of all existing microscopic particles could be determined, one could predict entirely the past and the future. That future is deterministic; not one based on freedom.

Quantum mechanics suggests a very different view. It posits an indeterminacy or spontaneity at the very heart of the natural world that from an evolutionary perspective opens an ontological ground for a world of freedom. Materialists, unable to move beyond an instrumental or technocratic epistemology, fail to recognize the transcending nature of our intelligence, constantly reaching beyond the object known to raise questions about the absolute that it already intuits.

Several psalms (Pss 93, 95, 96, 97, 98, 99) celebrate YHWH's lordship in virtue of his creative power. They proclaim him as king, ruling over all the gods, the earth and the seas, and all the earth's peoples. Originally used in the temple liturgy, they are often called enthronement psalms. This is the God of the Psalmist who rules over creation, a God of justice and everlasting love who renews the face of the earth and is coming to govern with justice and faithfulness (cf. Pss 96:13; 98:9). For in his care for the earth and its people, God's work's is not yet done. Christians will see these psalms fulfilled in Jesus.

3

A GOD WHO SAVES HIS PEOPLE

The Bible is the story of God's saving work, the God who created the heavens and the earth and all the earth's creatures, reaching into his world and into the lives of his people with his saving grace, that all might flourish and realize the mysterious divine purpose. The psalms celebrate God's work, bringing creation and salvation together in a way that expresses God's steadfast love. But they also celebrate God's people.

> When I look at your heavens, the work of your
> fingers,
> the moon and the stars that you have
> established;
> what are humans that you are mindful of them,
> mortals that you care for them? (Ps 8:3–4;
> NRSV)

Salvation, the abstract term for God's loving care for human beings, is a complex concept. We have seen some of this already. In this chapter, we focus on how the psalms proclaim God's saving work, in creation, on behalf of his chosen people, for those who prayerfully seek his face and those who long for justice. We begin with the context out of which the Psalmist's unique view of God emerged, the religion of their Canaanite neighbors.

Canaanite religion is difficult to reconstruct. Its pantheon was polytheistic, with multiple gods and goddesses. Their deities were often represented by figurines or statuettes, placed in shrines or sacred groves, often referred to in the Bible as the "high places." We've already seen some of their mythological epics expressive of their religious beliefs. The Baal Cycle tells of Baal's victory over Mot, the god of death; the Babylonian creation epic, *Enuma Elish* celebrates Marduk's victory over the monster goddess of the watery chaos, Tiamat; and Gilgamesh's search for eternal life is the subject of the epic that bears his name.

Much of Canaanite religion centered around two poles: a fertility cult invoking the storm god, Baal, important in the people's arid environment; and a cult of the dead. The souls of the dead were pacified with offerings of food and drink, to make sure they would not harm the living. Families venerated their own household gods, while each city had its own Baal. As the Baal Cycle taught, human beings were created to serve the gods, important for the well-being of the state.

Originally, YHWH was the tribal God of Israel, a God who accompanied his people. But one can trace a pattern in the biblical tradition where YHWH emerges as a supreme deity, ruling not just over the heavenly court or Israel, but all the nations and creation itself. The psalms reflect this development. While the Israelite religious tradition was in some ways shaped by that of their neighbors, their understanding of God and God's salvation was very different from that of the culture from which they came.

The word *salvation* has a multitude of connotations in the biblical tradition, both Old and New Testaments. The Hebrew word *yeshu'ah*, usually translated as salvation, comes from the Hebrew root *yš'*, signifying space, the freedom that comes from removing constriction. Salvation is also closely related to the idea of redemption.

In the Old Testament, it most often refers to God's deliverance of his people, whether through inspiring its leaders, military victories, or his righteous deeds. The great example of YHWH saving his people is the story of the exodus from Egypt, still commemorated in the annual Passover supper. Other examples include the return from exile in Babylon, or God's raising up judges to deliver people in times of crisis or delivering an individual from some illness or personal crisis.

In the New Testament, language about being saved has a secular origin, derived from the Greek *sōtēr*, "savior," *sōzein*, "save," and *sōtēria*, "salvation." The Synoptic Gospels refer to the miraculous cures or "saving" acts of Jesus that often conclude with Jesus saying, "Your faith has saved you." These cures or healings are signs of the saving power or reign of God breaking into a person's life through the ministry of Jesus, the one true savior.

In the Acts of the Apostles and the epistles, salvation stands for the works of God's mercy, God's transforming grace, and ultimately Christ's victory over sin and death in which we hope to share. Paul, faced with those he calls the "Judaizers," repeatedly stressed that God's salvation comes from faith in Christ, not from circumcision and observance of the law, "justification through faith." Let's now consider some of the psalms that celebrate God's salvation.

God Delivers Israel

Many of the psalms rehearse Israel's commemoration of God's saving acts. Of course, the paradigmatic example of God's saving Israel is their deliverance from bondage in Egypt as mentioned earlier, celebrated in many of the historical psalms. Psalm 105 is a musical recital of God's wonderful works, God's covenant with Abraham, the promise of the land of Canaan as their heritage, the story of Joseph, the people's migration to Egypt in time of famine and subsequent servitude. Then it tells the story of God raising up Moses, and Moses leading the Israelites out of bondage with signs and miracles from God, providing the Israelites with food in abundance and water in the desert to drink and giving them "the lands of the nations" (v. 44). The tone is one of praise of YHWH for his fidelity to his promises.

But Psalm 106 is very different; it is a confession of Israel's infidelity despite God's saving works, forgetting the God who saved them. The Israelites rebelled against the Most High at the Red Sea, and put God to the test in the desert; they were jealous of Moses, worshipped the image of a calf at Horeb, sacrificed to the idols of Canaan, and offered even their sons and daughters in sacrifice. Thus, they polluted the land with blood and became unclean by their acts. The psalm ends with a plea for God's salvation and promises to give thanks once more to God's holy name.

Psalm 78 is pedagogical; it reviews for future generations the story of God's saving acts, from Egyptian captivity to his sanctuary on Mount Zion and the accession of David as king. Despite God's mighty works, letting his anger loose against the Egyptians to secure their release, guiding them through the desert, parting the waters of the sea and leading them with a fiery light, giving them water from the rock and manna to eat—described in a lovely expression as "the bread of angels" (v. 25)—the people were not faithful. They refused to walk according to the law, forgetting God's mighty acts, and rebelling against him in the desert. They tested Moses, demanding the food they craved, and refusing to trust in God's saving power. Despite God's punishments, they continued to sin, flattering God with their mouths while continuing to lie with their tongues. Because of this, God turned away from the northern tribes, "the tribe of Ephraim," choosing instead Judah and Mount Zion, with David as shepherd.

Psalm 89 is a lament, revealing the very personal relationship between God and God's covenant with the Davidic dynasty. It begins as a song of praise: "I will sing of your mercy forever, LORD proclaim your faithfulness through all ages" (Ps 89:2). It praises God for his covenant with David, his work in creation, creating the heavens and the earth, crushing Rahab, exalting David and overcoming his enemies. But then it accuses God of renouncing the covenant, not supporting David's descendant in battle, letting his enemies to triumph, lamenting, "Where are your former mercies, Lord, that you swore to David in your faithfulness?" (Ps 89:50).

For the Psalmist, God's salvation does not come from military might, but from trust in the Lord: "A king is not saved by a great army, nor a warrior delivered by great strength. Useless is the horse for safety; despite its great strength, it cannot be saved" (Ps 33:16–17; cf. 44:6–8). It is this message that Israel so often failed to learn.

Psalm 137 is a deeply human postexilic lament, reflecting on the painful experience of the Babylonian captivity (597–538 BCE). The tone is bleak, reflecting the suffering of Israel in exile:

> By the rivers of Babylon
>   there we sat weeping
>   when we remembered Zion....
> For there our captors asked us
>   for the words of a song....
> But how could we sing a song of the LORD
>   in a foreign land?
> If I forget you, Jerusalem,
>   may my right hand forget.
> May my tongue stick to my palate
>   if I do not remember you. (Ps 137:1–6)

God's work in creation is also an example of salvation, as we noted earlier, dividing the waters and crushing Leviathan, the watery dragon of chaos (Ps 74:13). Psalm 136 brings together the two themes of creation and salvation, reviewing the saving history and completing each verse by proclaiming "his mercy endures forever."

But it is the poor—often expressed by the Hebrew word *'ānāwîm*, meaning those in serious need—and the oppressed who most needed God's salvation, a prominent theme in the psalms. Some examples: "For the needy will never be forgotten, nor will the hope of the afflicted ever fade" (Ps 9:19). "'Because they rob the weak, and the needy groan, I will now arise,' says the LORD; 'I will grant safety to whoever longs for it'" (Ps 12:5). Or "O Lord, who is like you, who rescue the afflicted from the powerful, the afflicted and needy from the despoiler?" (Ps 35:10). Psalm 72 says, "That he may defend the oppressed among the people, save the children of the poor and crush the oppressor" (v. 4), and again, "[He] rescues the poor when they cry out, the oppressed who have no one to help. He shows pity to the needy and the poor and saves the lives of the poor" (vv. 12–13). And always, God hears their cry (cf. Ps 69:33; also Pss 10; 34:17–18; 109:31; 140:12). Not so the cries of the wicked. The wicked will disappear, their swords will pierce their own hearts, and their arms will be broken; they will vanish like smoke and their future generations will be cut off (cf. Ps 37).

God's Steadfast Love

God's saving acts can also be personal, delivering an individual from personal experiences of distress, whether sickness, persecution, or even sin. Many of the psalms, even when they stand for the community of Israel, are written in the first person. They stand for individual members of the community who call upon God in the morning and confess his faithfulness at night (cf. Ps 92:3). The psalms show them praying for deliverance from their enemies, from the godless who oppress them, for health in sickness, or for forgiveness of their sins. They pray that God might shine his face upon them. Others ask for God's protection:

> Have mercy on me, God,
>   have mercy on me.
>   In you I seek refuge.
> In the shadow of your wings I seek refuge
>   till harm pass by. (Ps 57:1)

Some psalms are a confession of sin and plea for mercy, reflecting a remarkable personal honesty and self-awareness:

> Have mercy on me, God, in accord with your
>   merciful love;
>   in your abundant compassion blot out my
>   transgressions.
> Thoroughly wash away my guilt;
>   and from my sin cleanse me.
> For I know my transgressions;
>   my sin is always before me. (Ps 51:2–5)

But their relations with God are more than petitionary or confessional; one senses in the psalms a deep, personal relationship with God. The Psalmist is not afraid to argue with God, accusing God of hiding his face or forgetting his covenant (cf. Pss 13:1; 80; 89:38–51). He longs to experience the Lord's presence, to see God's face:

As the deer longs for streams of water,
so my soul longs for you, O God.
My soul thirsts for God, the living God.
When can I enter and see the face of God?
(Ps 42:2–3)

Nowhere is this loving relationship between YHWH and the faithful better expressed than with the Hebrew word *hesed.* The standard rendering is "steadfast love," though often it appears as mercy or loving kindness, depending on the scripture version. It appears 128 times in the psalms, as in: "Give thanks to the LORD for he is good, his mercy endures forever!" (Ps 107:1) or "As the heavens tower over the earth, so his mercy towers over those who fear him" (Ps 103:11). "The term stands for the total relationship of the Lord and his people: all his saving interventions, his goodness, the promises and the covenants."[1] God's love is unending.

In Psalm 136, both a hymn of praise and historical psalm, praising God for his saving acts in Israel's history in the form of a litany, *hesed* appears as a recurring response, "for his mercy endures forever." In the Jewish liturgy, the psalm is called the "Great Hallel," used at the morning sabbath service and at the Passover Seder.

One of the most famous in the Psalter is Psalm 23, a beautiful hymn expressing trust in YHWH as a gracious protector or "shepherd." The psalm is attributed to David, who proclaims that the LORD makes him lie down in green pastures, beside restful waters, restoring his soul. God protects him as he walks through even "the darkest valley," so that he fears no evil. Becoming the host, God prepares a table in the presence of his enemies, with oil for his head and an overflowing cup. The psalm concludes "Indeed, goodness and mercy will pursue me all the days of my life; I will dwell in the house of the LORD for endless days."

Psalm 103 praises God's for all his benefits and steadfast love. Though it reviews YHWH's saving acts in Israel's history, as in Psalm 23, there is a universal dimension to those who turn to the Lord in prayer.

> Bless the Lord, my soul;
> all my being, bless his holy name!
> Bless the Lord, my soul;
> and do not forget all his gifts,
> Who pardons all your sins,
> and heals all your ills,
> Who redeems your life from the pit,
> and crowns you with mercy and compassion,
> Who fills your days with good things,
> so your youth is renewed like the eagle's.
> (Ps 103:15)

Life beyond the Grave?

Israel's profound sense of YHWH's steadfast love speaks powerfully of their relationship with God. But did God's covenant relationship extend beyond this life? The Psalmist knows the frailty of human existence, frequently comparing the brief span of our days to God's eternity (cf. Ps 102:12–13); our days are like an herb or grass before the wind, we are but dust (Pss 90:5–6; 103:15–16). A further mystery is why those who do evil so often seem to prosper: "I saw the prosperity of the wicked. For they suffer no pain; their bodies are healthy and sleek. They are free of the burdens of life; they are not afflicted like others" (Ps 73:3–5). Implicit here is the question of God's justice.

Until late in Old Testament history, human destiny was seen as nothing more than an ultimate descent into Sheol, the underworld. Simply a synonym for death, Sheol was a shadowy realm or underworld, a place of silence and darkness. But worst of all, descending into Sheol meant the end of one's relationship with YHWH, for the dead could no longer praise him (Pss 6:6; 115:17). Conversely, the joy expressed in the psalms for a relationship with YHWH, even without belief in life after death, is eloquent testimony to the depth of Israel's faith and experience of God.

However, later in the Old Testament period, several clues emerge suggesting that death may not have the last word. One sign of hope surfaced during the efforts of Antiochus IV to unify his kingdom by stamping out Jewish religion, when Jews began dying for practicing their faith. The result was the introduction of apocalyptic thinking that saw God intervening in Israel's life and raising the just to life (cf. Dan 12:1–3). Wisdom 3:1–9 is another example, proclaiming that, "the souls of the just are in the hand of God, and no torment shall touch them" (Wis 3:1), a passage that may reflect Hellenic influence.

Joseph Ratzinger/Pope Benedict XVI sees another instance in some of the later psalms, a growing conviction that communion with God is stronger than death. Psalm 16, for example, proclaims:

> Therefore my heart is glad, my soul rejoices;
> my body also dwells secure,
> For you will not abandon my soul to Sheol,
> nor let your devout one see the pit.
> You will show me the path to life,
> abounding joy in your presence,
> the delights at your right hand forever.
> (Ps 16:9–11)

This psalm suggests that a faithful relationship with God will not be broken even by death. The second example is from Psalm 73, which contrasts the apparent success of the wicked with the person of faith who relies on God's guidance:

> With your counsel you guide me,
> and at the end receive me with honor.
> Whom else have I in the heavens?
> None beside you delights me on earth.
> Though my flesh and my heart fail,
> God is the rock of my heart, my portion
> forever. (Ps 73:24–26)

This tradition of a life beyond the grave remained controversial even in the time of Jesus, with the Pharisees believing in the resurrection and the Sadducees rejecting it (cf. Mark 12:18–27). Even today, determining the precise meaning of these psalms is difficult. Ratzinger sees it as a tradition growing in the late Old Testament period. He acknowledges that the text has both strengths and weaknesses. But he concludes that it is not based on any theory of the soul or idea of the resurrection, but on the experience of communion: "Looking on God, being with God: this is recognized as the point from which the ever-present, all devouring-menace of Sheol may be overcome."[2]

A Narrower View

Conservative evangelical theology has too often reduced the rich biblical concept of salvation to a narrow notion of "getting saved," the happy result of getting born again. By entering a personal relationship with Jesus, one's sins were "covered over," a forensic concept stemming from Luther. One of my teachers once described this as "the great cover-up theory." In much of evangelical theology, if one has been saved, they have gained a "certainty of salvation," a confidence of entering eternal life. But God's salvation is a much richer concept.

Evangelical theologian Scot McKnight acknowledges that much of evangelical theology stresses not Jesus's preaching about the kingdom of God, but Paul's teaching and the doctrine of justification by faith, for many, by "faith alone."[3] But this is to ignore the rich understanding of the kingdom of God in the biblical tradition. The original meaning of salvation, as we noted earlier, was political or historical, the liberation of Israel from bondage in Egypt, and—for much of the Old Testament—God's saving grace meant the rescue of his people by victory over their enemies. In the late post-exilic period, the idea of the resurrection of the dead or life after death in communion with YHWH entered in, as we have suggested.

That vision or hope was confirmed in the New Testament with the proclamation of the resurrection of Jesus, a hope in eternal life that we share. But the concept of salvation in the New Testament was much richer. God's salvation is exemplified or "enacted"—using Elizabeth Johnson's term—in Jesus's miracles and cures; he healed the sick, cleansed those suffering from leprosy or troubled by evil spirits, restoring them to their communities, and forgiving their sins.[4] From a Christian perspective, salvation means God's saving, transforming grace reaching into peoples' lives to bring health, wholeness, and communion with God and others. In his preaching, Jesus referred to this grace as the kingdom or reign of God.

A Contemporary Reflection

Karl Rahner describes grace as the free, self-communication of God, reaching its fullness in the Incarnation, this full union of the human and the divine in the person of Jesus. At the same time, the union of the divine and the human is the goal toward which every person, given the transcendental structure of human nature, is moving, though always dependent on one's openness to or cooperation with the divine. Thus, salvation means so much more than deliverance from sin. It cannot be reduced to "getting saved" and going to heaven, leading to the false view that we do not need to cooperate with God's grace.

Nor can faithful disciples simply overlook the social dimensions of Jesus's preaching of the kingdom of God. He came to proclaim good news to the poor, release of captives, and to let the oppressed go free (cf. Luke 4:18);

he called the poor and the hungry blessed (cf. Luke 6:20–21); and said that when we feed the hungry, give drink to the thirsty, welcome the stranger, clothe the naked, take care of the sick, and visit the imprisoned, all of this we do for him (cf. Matt 25:31–46). Thus, in reflecting on the saving grace of God, who the psalms tell us hears the voice of the poor, we should ask: "Who are the poor today?"

We live in a world with so many people marginalized, so much suffering, so many victims of violence and war. The divide between the wealthy and the very poor continues to increase, contributing to the present migration crisis. The International Organization for Migration's World Migration Report 2024 estimated the number of migrants worldwide as of October 2023 to be 281 million, with 117 million displaced by conflict, violence, disaster, and changing environments, the highest levels on record. Millions have been killed or have become part of the migration crisis owing to wars or political violence in Ukraine, the Middle East, South Sudan, and Haiti. This crisis has led to xenophobic attitudes and the rise of right-wing, nationalist movements aimed at ethnic, racial, and religious minorities in Europe and the United States.

Many other issues that victimize the vulnerable remain unaddressed. Women and children continue to be victims of sexual trafficking. Many children and young people are denied an education because of issues of poverty, gender, or refugee status. Many countries lack adequate health care. The global climate crisis adds to the number of refugees and contributes to hunger in many countries. It is estimated that 1.2 billion people will be displaced by 2050. According to UNICEF, some impoverished families are forcing their young female children into marriages in return for food.

In the United States, there is increasing racial tension. White supremacy remains a problem, and antisemitism is on the rise. An out-of-control gun culture led to 48,830 shooting deaths in 2021, the most recent year for which complete data is available. With handguns readily available, suicides counted for 54 percent of these deaths. In addition, 2,590 were children and teens under eighteen, including twenty-five children from mass shootings—often with assault rifles—in schools. When we reach out to the disadvantaged and the suffering, helping them to find hope, we can mediate God's saving grace, for God works through us to touch others.

Today, we are far more aware of the fragility of our beautiful earth—blue and white against the darkness of space—and the damage for which we are responsible. The Psalmist, celebrating in personal terms creation's sense for the active presence of the Creator, recognizes the unity between nature and the divine. Psalms 96 to 100 call on the earth and its creatures to sing praise to God. "The LORD is king; let the earth rejoice; let the many islands be glad" (97:1; cf. 96:1). "Let the rivers clap their hands, the mountains shout with them for joy, Before the Lord who comes, who comes to govern the earth" (98:8-9; cf. 65:13).

With the earth itself threatened, some new questions have arisen. Roland Murphy asks: Is creation irreversible, given the persistence of evil? Still, as he points out, the Psalmist has a confidence in the divine rule over creation.[5] And as we saw earlier, Paul's cosmic vision of salvation in Christ affects creation itself (cf. Rom 8:19–22).

In his beautiful encyclical *Laudato Si'*, Pope Francis stresses the interconnectedness of created reality, with all living creatures dependent on each other. He writes,

> As part of the universe, called into being by one Father, all of us are linked by unseen bonds and together form a kind of universal family, a sublime communion which fills us with a sacred, affectionate and humble respect. Here I would reiterate that "God has joined us so closely to the world around us that we can feel the desertification of the soil almost as a physical ailment, and the extinction of a species as a painful disfigurement." (*LS* 89)

Related by bonds of family and kinship, we have a responsibility for nature; we need to hear both the cry of the poor and the cry of the earth itself.

Joseph Ratzinger sees this cosmic dimension to salvation. In his book on eschatology, he writes, "The individual's salvation is whole and entire only when the salvation of the cosmos and all the elect has come to full fruition."[6]

Conclusion

We began this chapter with a brief discussion of how the Israelite understanding of the divine differed from the polytheistic, often violent religious views of their Canaanite neighbors. While their own religious tradition was influenced in some ways by the world they inhabited, their own understanding of their God was quite different.

YHWH, the God of Israel, developed from a tribal deity into the sovereign creator of the heavens and the earth and all their creatures, while the relation between the community of Israel and her God was both salvific and personal.

The psalms praise God for his mighty works on behalf of his people, but they also confess their frequent lapses and infidelity, begging him for mercy. Still, the psalms insist on God's fidelity to his covenant. Other psalms express the heartfelt prayers of individuals. They give voice to their petitions for God's saving grace on behalf of individuals and express their longings for a deeper relationship with YHWH, to experience his love and see his face.

We saw how the rich biblical idea of salvation has suffered a cultural reduction to a narrow, individualistic notion of "getting saved." Salvation means so much more than the forgiveness of our sins: It means God's grace, a share in God's life; freely bestowed, though always dependent on our free response. It cannot overlook the Psalmist's view that the God of Israel was a God who always hears the cry of the poor. Finally, God's salvation embraces not just us, but all creation.

4

PRAYING THE PSALMS

The psalms are at the heart of the Catholic Church's official prayer, variously called the Divine Office, the Canonical Hours, or the Breviary, and currently the Liturgy of the Hours. Christians from other churches also pray some of the "Hours." We will consider the Jewish and early Christian practice of shared prayer at fixed times of the day; the development of the monastic office, based largely on the Psalter; the emergence of the Roman Breviary in 1568; and Vatican II's reform of the Breviary leading to the Liturgy of the Hours.

The psalms were at the center of Israelite prayer, expressing the joy devout Israelites experienced in taking part in the temple services. As we saw earlier, to come into the temple was to come into God's presence among God's people. It was a sacred place, entered with songs of praise. But it is difficult to reconstruct the details of Jewish worship or what its practices were at the time of Christ, including daily public or private services.

There is general agreement that both Jews and Christians prayed at fixed times. Before the differences between the two traditions became clear, the earliest Christians continued to pray in the temple, while they gathered in their homes for the breaking of the bread, usually understood as Luke's term for the Eucharist (cf. Acts 2:46). Hellenistic Jewish Christians, however, moved quickly beyond the temple and its cult. Furthermore, it is not clear how Jewish practice influenced the development of the monastic office.

We know that, from the earliest days, Christians celebrated baptism and the Eucharist in their assemblies, and the author of Colossians gives us an example of their prayer from the sub-apostolic period: "Let the word of Christ dwell in you richly, as in all wisdom you teach and admonish one another, singing psalms, hymns, and spiritual songs with gratitude in your hearts to God. And whatever you do, in word or in deed, do everything in the name of the Lord Jesus, giving thanks to God the Father through him" (Col 3:16–17). Thus, Christians prayed the psalms from the beginning.

The Monastic Office

The early monks in the deserts of Palestine, Syria, and Egypt based their prayer on the Psalter, meditatively reading or reciting the psalms in their cells to lead them into more personal prayer and contemplation. An ancient tradition favored by St. Augustine interpreted the psalms christologically; most were seen as pointing to Christ. There are passages and psalms open to such reading; the Church has always heard them as expressing the voice of Christ (cf. Ps 22). Still, as Roland Murphy observes, "In Christian terms, it is the Father of Jesus Christ who is the focus of the Old Testament. Hence a merely Christocentric reading is incomplete; it does not grasp the psalms at the level on which they were written."[1]

Some of the early desert fathers and mothers could recite the entire Psalter from memory. Later, these monastics began reciting or chanting the psalms antiphonally in their churches, "in choir," fulfilling their duty to praise God. This became known as the *Opus Dei* or "work" of God. Following the Jewish practice (cf. Ps 92:2), they prayed at fixed hours, gathering early in the morning for Lauds and again in the evening for Vespers, today called Morning Prayer and Evening Prayer, respectively. Soon, they added a longer "hour" or assembly before dawn called Matins or Vigils, a period of psalms, hymns, readings from scripture, and quiet prayer. Later the minor hours of Terce, Sext, and None were added—the third, sixth, and ninth hour of the day—as well as Compline, a brief hour celebrated before retiring. It also became customary to chant "The Canticle of Mary" (cf. Luke 1:47–55) at Morning Prayer and "The Canticle of Zechariah" (cf. Luke 1:68–80) at Evening Prayer, and the Trinitarian doxology at the end of each psalm.

Thus developed the monastic office, the practice of gathering seven times a day (cf. Ps 119:164), in choir, a practice recommended by Hippolytus of Rome (d.c. 235). Indeed, the whole lives of monastics revolves around the

Opus Dei: the "work" or praise of God. Eleven chapters of St. Benedict's monastic rule are devoted to the celebration of the Divine Office, but chapter 19 shows a special concern for an awareness of the presence of God when in choir: "We believe that the divine presence is everywhere and that in every place the eyes of the Lord are watching the good and the wicked (Prov 15:3). But beyond the least doubt we should believe this to be especially true when we celebrate the divine office."

By the mid-fourth century, the bishop's church or cathedral began hosting a briefer version of the office, what became known as the cathedral office. This brief survey traces the development of the monastic office and ultimately the Roman Breviary, which was first published in Latin in 1568 as the *Breviarium Romanum*.[2] Members of the clergy and men and women religious are considered to have an obligation to pray daily at least parts of the Divine Office. Pope Pius XII authorized the development of a new translation of the psalms from the Hebrew and established a special commission to study a revision of the Breviary. Pope John XXIII implemented the revised version in 1960.

The Liturgy of the Hours

The Second Vatican Council initiated a reform of the Breviary, shortening it and making it available in vernacular languages. According to Vatican II's *Constitution on the Sacred Liturgy*, "Pastors of souls should see to it that the chief hours, especially Vespers, are celebrated in common in church on Sundays and the more solemn feasts. And the laity, too, are encouraged to recite the divine office, either with the priests, or among themselves, or even individually" (*SC* 100). Thus, the Council opened the Church's official liturgical prayer, newly named in 1971 as The Liturgy of the Hours, to lay men and women. Under Pope Paul VI, the Liturgy of the Hours was extended over a four-week cycle, adding an Office of Readings, consisting of three psalms and two readings, one from scripture and one from the Fathers of the Church or the canon of the saints. The present four-volume *Liturgy of the Hours* appeared in 1975, arranged according to the liturgical seasons: Advent, Lent, and the two volumes of Ordinary Time. There is currently another revised Liturgy of the Hours in preparation.

Praying the Psalms Today

Most monastic communities work through the entire Psalter in a week. Many contemplative communities begin their prayer with Vigils or Matins before dawn. Vigils usually has several groupings of psalms, antiphons, and scripture readings, called "nocturns." Vespers, toward evening, generally has three psalms. The minor hours are briefer.

But one does not have to be a cleric or religious to join in the church's public prayer. Many Christians pray the Liturgy of the Hours as members of Christ's body, joining with Christians everywhere praying for the Church and for the world. As St. Augustine says in his *Exposition on the Book of Psalms*, referring to Psalm 86, "It is our Lord Jesus Christ, the Son of God, who both prays for us, and prays in us, and is prayed to by us. He prays for us, as our Priest; He prays in us, as our Head; He is prayed to by us, as our God."

Some use the Liturgy of the Hours in the four volume or one volume versions; others use one of the shorter versions. Some turn to the Psalter itself, in a book of the psalms or simply turn to the psalms in their Bibles. Happily, the psalms are available in various formats. Helpful for travel is the online iBreviary, produced by the Custody of the Holy Land, a nongovernmental organization (NGO) that traces its roots to St. Francis of Assisi.

One should pray the Liturgy of the Hours with glad hearts. Psalm 95, the Invitatory for the beginning of the Office, calls for praise and thanksgiving in God's presence:

> O come, let us sing to the Lord;
> let us make a joyful noise to the rock of our salvation!
> Let us come into his presence with thanksgiving;
> let us make a joyful noise to him with songs of praise!
> For the Lord is a great God and a great King
> above all gods.
> In his hand are the depths of the earth;
> the heights of the mountains are his also.
> The sea is his, for he made it, and the dry land,
> which his hands have formed.

But the key is to move slowly through the text, not rushing to finish the passage, but pausing quietly wherever one finds fruit. Here the monastic practice of *lectio divina* (divine reading) can be especially helpful. It refers to a slow, meditative reading of scripture, not for study or analysis but simply to hear what God might be saying through the revelatory, biblical text. St. Ignatius of Loyola says something similar in his directions for prayer in the *Spiritual Exercises*, using the "Our Father" as an example: "During the contemplation on the 'Our Father,' if he finds in one or two words good matter for thought, relish, and consolation, he should be anxious to pass on, even though he spend the entire hour on what he has found."[3] But to pray fruitfully, one needs to bring an intentional awareness to the prayer, not rushing to finish. I once knew a priest who read Evening Prayer during the nightly news on TV. A rushed reading is far from the practice of *lectio divina*.

The rich imagery and poetry of the psalms, calling to mind God's creative work in shaping the universe and sustaining it, invites our wonder and praise. Like the Israelites of old, we experience joy in God's presence; we too trust in his faithfulness and mercy, his compassion and righteous judgment, knowing that evil never has the last word. The historical psalms invite us to reflect on our own personal histories, remembering where God has been present in special moments, moments of deep prayer or of sorrow for our failures and sins.

Most of all, like the Psalmist, we so often experience a longing for a deeper relationship with the God whose mystery we sense. St. Catherine of Siena once beautifully expressed this longing:

> It is the experience of God who cannot be known directly but in drawing near awakens in us a hunger that can never be stilled, a desire

> that can never be satisfied. You are a mystery as deep as the sea; the more I search, the more I find, and the more I find the more I search for you. But I can never be satisfied; what I receive will ever leave me desiring more. When you fill my soul I have an even greater hunger and I grow more famished for your light.[4]

Sometimes when we pray the psalms, we experience a particular psalm touching something deep within us; we are moved, filled with wonder, or joy, or sorrow. A new insight into our inner life is revealed, and perhaps a sense for God's nearness. That is the Spirit moving within us, speaking to us through the biblical text. God touches us through our affectivity or our imaginations. Afterward, it's good to reflect: Did the psalm speak to me in some way? How were we moved? What did I learn?

In its renewal of the liturgy of the Eucharist, Vatican II added a responsorial psalm to the readings, ideally to be sung between a cantor and the congregation. This should have made us more familiar with the psalms, and certainly the antiphonal responses—themselves verses from the psalms, whether recited or sung—often stay with us. They become part of our religious memory, and we sometimes find ourselves praying or mentally singing the antiphons. This, too, is a form of prayer when we find ourselves repeating quietly:

> The Lord is my shepherd, I shall not want.
> The Lord hears the cry of the poor.
> Happy are they who hope in the Lord.

My soul is thirsting for you, O Lord my God
To you O Lord, I lift up my soul.
Our help is from the Lord who made heaven
and earth.
Lord, let your face shine upon me.
The Lord is kind and merciful.

Conclusion

The Psalmists' understanding of God was a work still in progress. The Spirit was working in the Israelite community, enabling them to see more deeply into the mystery of the divine. They were not yet strict monotheists. Nor had they entirely moved beyond burnt offerings or animal sacrifices, but were moving in that direction. The temple was the House of the Lord, a sacred place. At the same time, they knew that God truly dwelt in the heavens; that is, beyond any limit of time or space (cf. Ps 139:7–12).

But Israel's God was not distant from his people. The psalms celebrate his closeness, his compassion and mercy. While many of the psalms were used in the temple liturgy, some were prayed by individuals, as is evident from their very personal language.

Some verses still make us cringe, as when the Psalmist, reflecting on the painful experience of the Babylonian captivity, says: "...blessed the one who pays you back what you have done us! Blessed the one who seizes your children and smashes them against the rock" (Ps 137:8–9). The verse is one of the most violent in the psalms. But what surfaces here is the profound grief of a people sorrowing in exile, the deeply human feelings that so often characterize the psalms. Some editors want to censor these more negative passages. But, as Roland Murphy argues, violence and revenge are part of life; we need to confront these same realities in the Bible.[5] Doing so reminds us of the stages in our own personal journeys.

The psalms proclaim the God who spread out the vastness of the heavens, filling it with stars and calling each one by name. This God fashioned the earth, sustaining it, sending the rains to make it fruitful, providing food for its creatures, creating men and women in his own image and likeness. Not a distant God, but one who chose a people to be his own, teaching them his ways, hearing the cries of their poor, promising to be with them.

The psalms proclaim God's hand in our creation, forming us in our mothers' wombs, filling our hearts with his love. Each human life, created in God's image, is sacred. Though our days are numbered, our lives a mere breath, and our existence fragile, God is never far from us. We cannot hide from God's spirit. When we sin, the psalms voice our pleas for forgiveness, reminding us of God's faithfulness and compassion. While the Psalmist clearly does not see a life beyond this one, a variant tradition says that communion with God cannot be broken, for God will not give up his faithful to Sheol, but will be their portion forever.

The psalms have nourished Christian prayer from the earliest days, from the fathers and mothers of the desert to men and women of today, whether in religious communities or among the laity. Beyond the hymns, poetry, and prayers, the psalms point beyond to their God, to our God, with his everlasting love.

NOTES

Introduction

1. See Sigmund Mowinckel, *The Psalms in Israel's Worship* (Malden, MA: Blackwell, 1962).

2. Ambrose of Milan, *Explanation of the Psalms*, 1,4.7–8.

3. See Christian Smith and Melinda Lundquist Denton, *Soul Searching: The Religious and Spiritual Lives of American Teenagers* (New York: Oxford University Press, 2005), 162–63.

4. See Charles Taylor, *A Secular Age* (Cambridge, MA: The Belknap Press of Harvard University, 2007).

Chapter 1

1. Roland E. Murphy, *The Gift of the Psalms* (Peabody, MA: Hendrickson Publishers, 2000), 143.

2. Murphy, *Gift of the Psalms*, 140.

3. Anselm, *Proslogion*, 16.

4. Rudolf Otto, *The Idea of the Holy* (New York: Oxford University Press, 1958).

5. Karl Rahner, "Thomas Aquinas on the Incomprehensibility of God," *Journal of Religion* (supplement) 58 (1978): 107–25.

6. Rahner, "Thomas Aquinas on the Incomprehensibility of God," S. 123.

7. Thomas Merton, *New Seeds of Contemplation* (New York: New Directions, 1961), 240.

8. Thomas Keating, "Practicing Centering Prayer," in *The Diversity of Centering Prayer*, ed. Gustave Reininger (New York: Continuum, 1999), 11–26.

9. Ignatius of Loyola, *The Spiritual Exercises of St. Ignatius*, trans. Anthony Mottola, introduction by Robert W. Gleason (Garden City, NY: Doubleday, 1964), 71.

10. Mother Teresa, *Mother Teresa: Come Be My Light*, ed. Brian Kolodiejchuk (Garden City, NY: Doubleday, 2007), 1–2.

Chapter 2

1. Roland E. Murphy, *The Gift of the Psalms* (Peabody, MA: Hendrickson Publishers, 2000), 172.

2. Ignatius of Loyola, *The Spiritual Exercises of St. Ignatius*, trans. Anthony Mottola, introduction by Robert W. Gleason (Garden City, NY: Doubleday, 1964), 104.

3. See Karl Rahner, "Christology within an Evolutionary View of the World," in *Foundations of Christian Faith: An Introduction to the Idea of Christianity* (New York: Crossroad, 1982), 178–203.

4. John F. Haught, *Making Sense of Evolution: Darwin, God, and the Drama of Life* (Louisville, KY: Westminster John Knox Press, 2010), 138–39.

5. Elizabeth A. Johnson: *Ask the Beasts: Darwin and the God of Love* (New York: Bloomsbury, 2014), 196.

6. See Michael Cook, *Trinitarian Christology: The Power That Sets Us Free* (Mahwah, NJ: Paulist Press, 2010).

Chapter 3

1. Roland E. Murphy, *The Gift of the Psalms* (Peabody, MA: Hendrickson Publishers, 2000), 45.

2. Joseph Ratzinger, *Eschatology: Death and Eternal Life*, 2nd ed. (Washington, DC: Catholic University of America Press, 1988), 88–90.

3. See Scot McKnight, "Jesus vs. Paul," *Christianity Today* 54, no. 12 (2020): 24–29.

4. Elizabeth A. Johnson, *Consider Jesus: Waves of Renewal in Christology* (New York: Crossroad, 2001), 54.

5. Murphy, *Gift of the Psalms*, 42–44.

6. Ratzinger, *Eschatology*, 238.

Chapter 4

1. Roland E. Murphy, *The Gift of the Psalms* (Peabody, MA: Hendrickson Publishers, 2000), 66.

2. For more on the history, see Robert Taft, *The Liturgy of the Hours in East and West: The Origins of the Divine Office and Its Meaning for Today* (Collegeville, MN: Liturgical Press, 1986).

3. Ignatius of Loyola, *The Spiritual Exercises of St. Ignatius*, trans. Anthony Mottola, introduction by Robert W. Gleason (Garden City, NY: Doubleday, 1964), 107.

4. Catherine of Siena, *Gratiarum actio ad Trinitatem*, cap. 167.

5. See Murphy, *Gift of the Psalms*, 50.

SELECTED BIBLIOGRAPHY

Primary Sources

Ambrose of Milan, *Explanation of the Psalms.*

Anselm. *Proslogion.*

Catherine of Siena. *Gratiarum actio ad Trinitatem.*

Ignatius of Loyola. *The Spiritual Exercises of St. Ignatius.* Translated by Anthony Mottola. Introduction by Robert W. Gleason. Garden City, NY: Doubleday, 1964.

Mother Teresa. *Mother Teresa: Come Be My Light.* Edited with commentary by Brian Kolodiejchuk. Garden City, NY: Doubleday, 2007.

Secondary Sources

Cook, Michael. *Trinitarian Christology: The Power That Sets Us Free.* Mahwah, NJ: Paulist Press, 2010.

Haught, John F. *Making Sense of Evolution: Darwin, God, and the Drama of Life.* Louisville, KY: Westminster John Knox Press, 2010.

Johnson, Elizabeth A. *Ask the Beasts: Darwin and the God of Love*. New York: Bloomsbury, 2014.

———. *Consider Jesus: Waves of Renewal in Christology*. New York: Crossroad, 2001.

Keating, Thomas. "Practicing Centering Prayer." In *The Diversity of Centering Prayer*, edited by Gustave Reininger. New York: Continuum, 1999.

McKnight, Scot. "Jesus vs. Paul." *Christianity Today* 54, no. 12 (2020): 24–29.

Merton, Thomas. *New Seeds of Contemplation*. New York: New Directions, 1961.

Mowinckel, Sigmund. *The Psalms in Israel's Worship*. Malden, MA: Blackwell, 1962.

Murphy, Roland E. *The Gift of the Psalms*. Peabody, MA: Hendrickson Publishers, 2000.

Otto, Rudolf. *The Idea of the Holy*. New York: Oxford University Press, 1958.

Rahner, Karl. "Christology within an Evolutionary View of the World." In *Foundations of Christian Faith: An Introduction to the Idea of Christianity*. New York: Crossroad, 1982.

———. "Thomas Aquinas on the Incomprehensibility of God." *Journal of Religion* (supplement) 58 (1978): 107–25.

Ratzinger, Joseph. *Eschatology: Death and Eternal Life*, 2nd ed. Washington, DC: Catholic University of America Press, 1988.

Smith, Christian, and Melinda Lundquist Denton. *Soul Searching: The Religious and Spiritual Lives of American Teenagers*. New York: Oxford University Press, 2005.

Taft, Robert. *The Liturgy of the Hours in East and West: The Origins of the Divine Office and Its Meaning for Today*. Collegeville, MA: Liturgical Press, 1986.

Taylor, Charles. *A Secular Age*. Cambridge, MA: The Belknap Press of Harvard University, 2007.